Under God's Umbrella

Under God's Umbrella

A Pilgrimage through Life

Robert Mann Hartley

Charleston, SC
www.PalmettoPublishing.com

Under God's Umbrella

Copyright © 2022 by Robert Mann Hartley

First Edition

Hardcover ISBN: 979-8-8229-0047-9

Paperback ISBN: 979-8-8229-0048-6

Dedication

I WOULD LIKE TO dedicate the telling of my story to our four grandchildren:

Katherine Iris Hartley

William Peyton Hartley (right),
Robert Turner Hartley (left),
Sinclair Anne Hartley (middle)

MY STORY IS PART of their heritage and the heritage of the generations beyond them. My wife of fifty-two years, Nancy (Nancy Eyre Cheetham Hartley); our two sons, Rob and Jimmy (Robert Eyre Hartley and James Peyton Hartley); and their wives, Sabrina and Caroline (Sabrina Pianka Hartley and Caroline Goldston Hartley), are part of this history, and they know much of it well. I would like my grandchildren also to have a glimpse of my story. And what better way to do that than for me to tell it? This is part of my legacy to them.

I love these grandchildren with all my heart, as I do my sons, daughters-in-law, siblings, and all my family who helped shape me and have been a part of this story. A special thanks to Nancy, who helped me pull this anthology together.

Soli Deo Gloria, Granddaddy
Christmas, 2022

Contents

Prologue

"What should my life have looked like?" This is one of those first-order questions of life. Since I am anchored in a relationship with my Creator, I think a better way to ask the question is "What has been God's good and perfect will for my life?"

Looking back, I know my life has aligned with God's will for me imperfectly at best. As Saint Paul writes, "for all have sinned and fall short of the glory of God."[1] Such is the condition of us fallen human beings. However, without a doubt, what has been pleasing to God are the times I have sought His direction and purpose for my life and moved forward on my pilgrimage in the guidance and power of His Holy Spirit.

I have come to know that the only perfection any of us can have in this life is to be found in Christ, the only perfect Man. The perfect righteousness of Christ imputed to me is my only hope for a life perfect enough to come into the presence of our Heavenly Father at my last day. This makes my relationship with Christ the most precious thing about this story. This is what Jesus is saying in His parable of the hidden treasure and the parable

---

1 Romans 3:23.

of the pearl of great value in Matthew 13.[2] The good news is that my earthly pilgrimage, albeit flawed, is perfectly pleasing to God because of my relationship with Him in Jesus.

Thus, I can say that I have found the pearl of great price, and I believe that the trajectory of my life has always been Godward, even in the not-so-good times. It is therefore appropriate that I choose to tell my story by celebrating the good moments and allowing the not so good moments to remain covered by the blood of the Lamb[3] and hidden in Christ forever,[4] as Scripture tells us.

Through this autobiography, I have developed a deeper sense of thankfulness to God for how gracious and patient He has been toward me throughout the years. Since grade school, I have known, almost by heart, a prayer in the Daily Offices in *The Book of Common Prayer* known as the General Thanksgiving. The prayer says, "Give us such an awareness of your mercies, that with truly thankful hearts we may show forth your praise, not only with our lips, but in our lives, by giving up ourselves to your service, and by walking before you in holiness and righteousness all our days."[5]

I am indeed thankful that God has given me life and all the wonderful people who have been in my life. I am thankful for my parents who raised me; for Nancy, who sustains me; and for my children and grandchildren, who bring me joy every day.

---

2   Matthew 13:44–46. The parable of the hidden treasure: "The kingdom of heaven is like treasure hidden in a field, which a man found and covered up. Then in his joy he goes and sells all that he has and buys that field." The parable of the pearl of great value: "Again, the kingdom of heaven is like a merchant in search of fine pearls, who, on finding one pearl of great value, went and sold all that he had and bought it."

3   Ephesians 1:7.

4   Colossians 3:3.

5   *The Book of Common Prayer* 2019, Daily Office of Morning Prayer, according to the use of the Anglican Church in North America, page 25.

Part I

The Younger Years

Chapter 1

The Joys of Growing Up in Mount Pleasant

I was born November 18, 1947, and given the name Robert Mann Hartley. I was named for my mother's father, Robert Friday Mann. My grandfather was called Rob, as I am. I am honored to carry his name as well as his nickname. The name Robert has propagated widely throughout the Mann clan in the subsequent four generations.

Robert (Rob) Friday Mann

MY GRANDFATHER IS BURIED at Bethel Methodist Church, Bethel Community, Fairfield County, South Carolina, which is just upstate from Columbia, South Carolina. His wife, Eva McFadden Mann, a sweet and gentle woman I remember well from my childhood, was buried alongside him in a graveyard filled with Manns. The family has been there since the land grant years of colonial South Carolina.[6]

An early memory of my grandmother, whom we called Ms. E, is my coming into her bedroom at bedtime to find her sitting on the side of her bed, her back as straight as an arrow and her Bible in her lap. Even though I was unable to comprehend much at that tender age, I remember this because I knew I wanted whatever my dear grandmother had at that moment.

My parents are Evelyn Mann Hartley and Peyton Carsten Hartley.

---

6 Land grants in the colonial period in South Carolina were made by the king's officials beginning about 1730.

DAD WAS RAISED IN Charleston, South Carolina, and attended the College of Charleston, earning a degree in chemistry. Mom grew up in Fairfield County and in Columbia.

Mom and Dad were in the process of moving from Columbia to the Charleston area at the time of my birth. Dad was already working in Charleston and recounted the drive back to Columbia on the stormy night I arrived. They initially rented a house on the corner of Venning and Church Street in Mount Pleasant. Extraordinarily, I have memories of that house, playing in the yard and in the Bagwell's and Plowden's yards next door. This constitutes some of my earliest memories of childhood. Dad and Mom soon bought a house a block and a half away at 410 Church Street.

Me and my brother, Danny

MOUNT PLEASANT IS NESTLED on the eastern rim of Charleston Harbor. It was a small, quiet fishing and farming village in those days. Everything was in easy bicycle range for us kids. My best friend then and now is Durst Payne. We were different in many ways, as this picture of Durst's mother attempting to take our picture might suggest. We were different, but I could not have enjoyed any friendship more.

Durst is the one throwing something at his mother.

DURST LIVED TWO BLOCKS away from us and just back from a high bluff overlooking Charleston harbor. I have wonderful memories of the endless opportunities this bluff and waterfront afforded us. There was a Civil War gun emplacement, which was, of course, intriguing, but the two great attractions were Mr. Dupre's dock that gave us access to the harbor and the rowboat belonging to Durst's father that stayed in the marsh below the bluff.

That rowboat was an old, heavy wooden boat, quite a challenge for two small boys to manage, but once the tide lifted it out of the mud and marsh, it was an amazing source of freedom and exploration. We would travel great distances in that boat; even crossing the main shipping channel of Charleston Harbor to Castle Pinckney seemed undaunting (Castle Pinckney was part of the pre-Civil War harbor defenses, which had been long since abandoned). And then there were Shem Creek, Crab Bank, and Hog Island to explore. Our parents, who have long since departed this life, would have been surprised, even a bit horrified, to hear about some of our exploits.

Much fishing, crabbing, and shrimping (once we were big enough to handle a cast net) were done from this old rowboat. Fishing and crabbing along the banks of Shem Creek were always good. This was because of the shrimp boats that occupied the creek providing plenty of food from the culling of their daily catch. The Old Bridge (an abandoned bridge, which is still there to this day, at one time tied Mount Pleasant to Sullivan's Island and Fort Moultrie) was a delightful place to ride our bikes with our fishing poles on the back. Fort Moultrie, part of the harbor defenses and decommissioned after World War II, was a wonderful place to explore—although, in hindsight, a bit dangerous. We seemed to have survived it all, however.

In the summers, we would be sent out of the house after breakfast, have a peanut butter and jelly sandwich at whoever's house we happened to be at lunchtime, and expected to be home in time for supper. This allowed for long summer bicycle treks to places like Sullivan's Island, the truck farming fields past the edge of town, and even to what seemed like the edge of the earth, Christ Church and Gregory's store.

Christ Church was a small colonial era Anglican church, which today has grown into a sprawling East Cooper church. My grandparents (Daniel Peyton Hartley and Louise Tiedeman Hartley) and my parents, Peyton and Evelyn, are buried at Christ Church, just several yards away from the colonial-era church building. Nancy and I intend to be buried in that family plot—as do my brother, Dan (Daniel Peyton Hartley II); his wife, Pat (Patricia Fryfogle Hartley); my sister, Alice (Alice Randolph Hartley Myers); and her husband, Johnny (John David Myers).

Christ Church, Colonial Era Building

A FAVORITE SUMMER PASTIME was swimming in Hobcaw Creek at Bertha and Joe Cain's. Joe taught us boys about many things, such as deer hunting, vegetable gardening, and the fine art of wood chopping. Joe had us convinced that cutting and hauling firewood with him on Saturdays was a fun thing to do. Joe and Bertha had no children of their own but were like second parents to many of us kids around town. Joe was also a pillar of Saint Andrew's Church, where he often rotated through the junior warden position (caring for the facilities), something he was good at and loved doing. Looking back, I see that Joe modeled for me the Christian virtue of generosity and how to live a life that honors God. Joe and Bertha provided some of my fondest and richest memories of my growing-up years.

Me (left) and Durst (right) at Hobcaw Creek

ANOTHER MEMORY I HAVE of my summers in Mount Pleasant is, after having run around Mount Pleasant barefoot all week, how odd it felt to put on shoes to go to church on Sundays. Attending Saint Andrew's Church on Sundays was regular and consistent, and not going was never an option to our mother. As a family, we would always honor the Lord on the Lord's Day.

Saint Andrews Church

We lived two blocks away from the church, and walking was almost always the mode of transportation, even on chilly winter mornings. When I was old enough to acolyte, I would often be assigned to the 8:15 a.m. service. My mother would send me out the door at 7:30 without breakfast because she believed we should honor the church's practice of fasting before receiving Holy Communion. Given my empty stomach and the length of time that the 1928 prayer book kept one on his knees, I regularly felt woozy and wondered if I was going to faint. As an acolyte in the chancel, I would not dare think of leaning back onto the pew. I am sure Mr. Caitlin, our priest, would have preferred that to my falling over.

Alice (left), me (center), and Danny (right)

Alice

MIDDAY SUNDAY DINNER WITH my parents; my brother, Danny; and my sister, Alice; was always a special time. Mom was a great cook, and there was always a lot of food. At all the meals, my father would ask the blessing so quickly and quietly that once when asked what he said, he responded, "I wasn't talking to you anyway." No one asked him that question again because they knew the answer would be the same.

I don't know whether to judge my early childhood as normal or abnormal, but I do know it was a wonderful time for me.

Chapter 2

Glimpses of God

My first glimpses of God were conveyed to me by my mother. Ebbie was a loving, nurturing lady, although at times she was a force of nature to be reckoned with. My older brother, Danny, dubbed her "Hurricane Evelyn." She instilled in us the fear of immediate and considerable discipline for all transgressions, large or small. Nonetheless, she showed me what it meant to love God and love family. These many years later, I can clearly see that she modeled for me a relationship with God upon which I could not only base my behavior but also draw my very identity. Momma and Daddy, along with my family, showed me the importance and meaning of God and family.

My father was a hardworking and wise man. His spirituality was not as overt as my mother's, but he taught me much about living life God's way. I am very thankful for this and for his example of what it means to be a father. Among his attributes was his working hard for his family, and he made great sacrifices to see to it that us kids received a good start in our lives and, most importantly, that we received an education.

In World War II, Dad was in the Eighty-Second Airborne Division, 504th Infantry Regiment. He fought in Italy,[7] Holland, and the Battle of the Bulge in Belgium, and he entered Germany with his regiment in 1945. The Eighty-Second Airbourne participated in the famous and harrowing crossing of the Waal River, Holland, as part of Operation Market Garden[8] and the bloody battle to block the German general Joachim Peiper from pushing out of the north side of the pocket in the Battle of the Bulge. By the end of the battle to stop *Kampfgruppe* (battle group) Peiper, my father was commanding his company as the only officer to have survived.[9]

Dad, WWII

---

7   Frank van Lunteren, *Spearhead of the Fifth Army: The 504th Parachute Infantry Regiment in Italy, from the Winter Line to Anzio* (Havertown, PA: Casemate Publishers, 2016).

8   van Lunteren, *The Battle of the Bridges: The 504th Parachute Infantry Regiment in Operation Market Garden* (Havertown, PA: Casemate Publishers, 2014).

9   van Lunteren, *Blocking Kampfgruppe Peiper: The 504th Parachute Infantry Regiment in the Battle of the Bulge* (Havertown, PA: Casemate Publishers, 2015).

DAD WAS AWARDED TWO Purple Hearts, and he never seemed to fully recover from a wound to the neck. He struggled with health issues throughout my growing-up years perhaps because of that wound.

My father grew up through the Great Depression of the 1930s. His ethic was to work hard and be frugal with money. These are attributes that I believe he passed on to me, albeit my frugality does not hold a candle to his. To this day, my brother likes to remind me that I tend to be "over economical" (i.e., cheap) at times. He says it is that I have "too much Tiedeman in me," referring to the German frugality on my Grandmother Hartley's side of the family. I'm proud to say that it's just a bit of Dad coming out in me.

My father died in 1979 at the age of sixty-three, which is much younger than I am today. Mom and Dad visited Nancy; Robin, our first son (Robert Eyre Hartley); and me in Charlotte just weeks before his death. Jimmy, our second son (James Peyton Hartley), was only weeks from being born, and my father died without meeting this his fourth grandchild.

I remember some of the conversations I had with him on that visit, and I could hear his pleasure and satisfaction that his three children—Dan, Alice, and me—were well established in life and prospering. I don't believe there was anything in life more important to him than that.

There were three institutions in my growing-up years in Mount Pleasant that greatly contributed to my formation: Saint Andrew's Church, Porter Military Academy (later Porter-Gaud School), and Kanuga Conference Center. They each contributed to my formation in Christ and gave me glimpses of what it meant to live life under the umbrella of God's grace.

Saint Andrew's was situated in the heart of the old village of Mount Pleasant. In the 1800s, it served as a chapel of ease for the families of planters and plantation owners, who were sent to places like Mount Pleasant to catch a sea breeze and thus escape mosquitoes, malaria, and other maladies that plagued the countryside in the summer.

Saint Andrew's provided depth and clarity to the faith that I knew my mother felt so deeply and shared with me, and eventually that faith became my own as I was nurtured in that church family. There were many people at Saint Andrew's who shepherded me in one way or another—from the rector, The Reverend Llewellyn Catlin, to the array of Sunday school teachers and youth leaders I had during those years.

My brother Danny and I attended Porter Military Academy. I count Porter among one of the greatest blessings of my growing-up years, and I understand the sacrifices my mom and dad made in sending us there. I received an excellent education; I didn't realize to what extent until I went off to Clemson University. I felt very prepared for the academic rigors of pursuing my goal of earning an electrical engineering degree.

The Porter Military Academy was founded by the Reverend Doctor Anthony Toomer Porter after the Civil War when Charleston was destitute and many boys had been left orphaned by that terrible war. Dr. Porter was the rector of the Church of the Holy Communion, just three blocks up Ashley Avenue from a United States arsenal that occupied an entire city block in Charleston. The arsenal had become obsolete and unused. Dr. Porter boarded a train to Washington, DC, to make a case with the War Department that this property should be turned into a school for boys. Amazingly, General William Tecumseh Sherman—an educator himself and whose troops during the Civil War had so ravaged the deep South just years prior—became Dr. Porter's champion in starting a school on that property. In the century and a half since, the Episcopal Church developed Porter Military Academy, now Porter-Gaud, into a top-rated school. I'm blessed to have attended there.

Besides my academic formation, Porter also contributed to my spiritual formation. It dovetailed nicely with my growing up at Saint Andrew's Church. I have vivid memories of being in chapel every morning from grade school on into high school. The chapel was a Civil War-era brick building that always seemed colder inside than outside in the winter. We would kneel on its cold floors and sit in its hard, wooden pews; nonetheless, I have fond memories of those times. I don't remember readings or homilies, but I learned well the ancient prayers of the church. Most of all, I remember encountering God in that place. The service was always the Daily Office of Morning Prayer from the 1928 *Book of Common Prayer*. Morning Prayer became a comfortable and familiar friend of my youth.

A third institution that was formative for me in my growing up years was Kanuga Conference Center. Our family would regularly rent a cabin for a week in the mountains there. This is a place that our children and grandchildren also know well. At an exceedingly early age, I remember cane pole fishing with my older brother and father in Kanuga Lake just below Kanuga Lodge. We used poles given to my brother and me by my Aunt Alice (Alice Randolf Hartley Pane, one of my father's sisters). This was in the early 1950s, and I'm amazed how vivid this memory is to me to this day.

I attended other camps and conferences over the years, but Kanuga was the closest to my heart. I attended the Young People's (YP) Conference for a series of years and eventually worked as a kitchen helper at Kanuga in the summer between my junior and senior years in high school. Interestingly, our son Jimmy also worked in the kitchen at Kanuga between his junior and senior years in high school.

The tradition continued with Nancy and me taking our boys to Kanuga summer after summer. Jimmy and his wife, Caroline (Caroline Goldston Hartley), are continuing the tradition to this day, and we have been renting a cabin at Kanuga with them in recent summers. That is four generations of Hartleys who love Kanuga. Great memories there for us all!

KANUGA BECAME FOR ME what the ancient Celtic church called a "thin place," which is where the fabric between heaven and earth is drawn so thinly that one can almost reach through and touch the face of God.

For years, I have used Kanuga as a spiritual retreat. On the far side of the lake sits a bench on the edge of the trail behind the large, iconic Kanuga cross. The bench is peacefully and beautifully shrouded in a tunnel of mountain laurel, and it became a special place for me to commune with God and offer up both my joys and struggles.

Today, my favorite thing to do at Kanuga is rise at dawn and walk to that bench to visit with the Lord, inviting one of the Jimmy's sons to come with me (and hopefully also Sinclair, his daughter, when she is older). Amazingly, my grandsons almost always say yes. We have come to call it the God Bench. My discussions with the boys have always been deep, insightful, enjoyable, heartwarming, and mostly about God. There is a bench we come to before reaching the God Bench that the grandsons now call the Devil Bench. They throw sticks at it as they run by to get to the God Bench. It sounds delightfully metaphorical.

The God Bench

Chapter 3

Fascination with Math and Science—Another Glimpse of God

From junior high school on, I had been drawn toward the priesthood as a life calling. God and church were central to my life then as is now. I had good role models in the church, such as Mr. Catlin our rector at Saint Andrew's through those years. I even attended a diocesan vocation conference at Saint Jude's Church, Walterboro, to check it out at bit.

High School Years

HOWEVER, I WAS ALSO irresistibly drawn toward physics, and nothing fascinated me more than one of the fundamental forces of the universe: electromagnetism. It was in the eleventh grade that I firmly decided I wanted to study electrical engineering.

So what happened to the call toward the priesthood? It was, for sure, overshadowed by my interest in science, but I also did a bit of rationalizing to help it along. I conveniently became disillusioned with the apparent hypocrisy in the church, and it would be another decade before I would come to understand that one should not be surprised at the church's flaws; after all, in Mark 2:17, Jesus says, "Those who are well have no need of a physician, but those who are sick. I came not to call the righteous, but sinners."[10]

Nonetheless, I did question whether I had turned my back on what God really wanted me to do. I was to discover, decades later, that patience is one of God's great attributes. This was when I would once again hear a call to the priesthood. This time I would answer in the affirmative.

I was to discover that science gave me yet another glimpse into the mind of God. The subatomic world is full of mysteries, God's mysteries. Particle physicists cracking open protons with modern particle colliders are continuing to uncover new things about God's creation and how it works, and in the process, discovering even more surprises about His creation than they solved. I am reminded of Carey Landry's song "God Is a Surprise."[11]

I mentioned in a previous chapter about early morning walks at Kanuga to the God Bench on the far side of the lake. When my grandson William was ten years old, he and I talked about these fundamental building blocks of God's universe. I was amazed at William's interest and his ability, at least to some degree, to comprehend such abstract ideas. We talked about his generation having much yet to discover. I will always cherish that conversation with William that morning.

---

10   Mark 2:17, English Standard Version.

11   Carey Landry, "God Is a Surprise." Song lyrics and a performance can be found online at https://www.youtube.com/watch?v=a_vVoTvwLP4.

And who knows what God has yet for us to discover? When I was studying electrical engineering at Clemson, the textbooks listed electrons, protons, and neutrons as the fundamental building blocks of the universe, but today we know that is not true. We now talk about quarks, gluons, and such as being the even smaller building blocks from which protons and neutrons are composed. The complexity, intricacy, and incredible design of the material world is still beyond our full comprehension, as is the Mind of God.

The fact that the Mind of God is partly revealed to us through our exploration of the design and workings of His creation is not new. To me, this is intuitively obvious, and the psalmist is correct in writing "The heavens declare the glory of God, and the firmament shows his handiwork."[12] The thirteenth Century Dominican friar and priest, Thomas Aquinas, presented his case for this in what he called his cosmological argument for God (i.e. natural revelation) in his classic work, *Summa Theologica*.[13] A good contemporary source for exploring God's revelation of Himself in nature is Stephen Meyer's book, *Return of the God Hypothesis: Three Scientific Discoveries that Reveal the Mind Behind the Universe*.[14]

This became an important facete in my fascination with physics, both in cosmology (the study of God's creation on the macro-scale of the entire universe) and particle physics (the study of the of the smallest building blocks of creation). I have observed modern physicist's complex struggles in trying to explain the universe without invoking a Designer, and it always leads my mind back to a principle known as Occam's Razor attributed to the Franciscan friar, William of Occam. Simply stated Occam's Razor is that the simplest answer with the fewest assumptions is the best one.

---

12   Psalm 19, verse 1, Coverdale Translation.

13   Aquinas (c. 1225-1274), *Summa Theologica*. A good contemporary translation is by the Fathers of the English Dominican Fathers, Coyote Canyon Press, 2018.

14   Return of the God Hypothesis: Three Scientific Discoveries that Reveal the Mind behind the Universe, HarperCollins Publishers, New York, 2021.

Part II

The Formative Years

Chapter 4

The Amazing Clemson Years

My drift away from God was considerable during my Clemson University years. They were fun and rebellious years, and I was not particularly interested in complying with what I knew in my heart my life should look like. I justified it philosophically and spiritually by adopting a sort of deism in which God was not involved. God gave me a life with which I was to find my own way and make the most of it. My life was a micro-version of watchmaker analogy, which is that God wound up the universe and is letting it run. I would soon enough get over this because, as deism has been proven throughout history, it was an irrational belief, albeit convenient to me for a time. Furthermore, it was contrary to the God I had come to know in my youth, a God willing enough to be involved in my life and rescue me from myself by coming to me in the person of Jesus.[15]

In my junior year I met Nancy. She was attending Limestone College in upstate South Carolina, not far from Clemson. I invited her over to a football game and dance. Nancy, a cute young lady from Aiken, South Carolina, captured my interest immediately, and

---

15   Philippians 2:2–5, Galatians 4:4–5.

my heart was soon to follow. She was good for me, and I knew it. Nancy and I dated for the next two years.

WHEN I WOULD VISIT her at Limestone, it was not unusual for me to help her with her math studies, something I was good at, but she found a bit bewildering. She was an art major. The summer between my junior and senior years—while at Reserve Officers' Training Corps (ROTC) summer camp at Fort Bragg, North Carolina—I visited Nancy at Limestone on weekend leave. I once helped her stretch canvases for her art projects, and I remember what a comfortable and delightful weekend that was for me.

I enjoyed my studies at Clemson. The freshman and sophomore years were loaded with basic math and science courses to prepare us for the more advanced engineering courses of my junior and senior years. Physics was my favorite course series. I had taken twenty credit hours of physics in my first two years. I also had nearly as many hours of mathematics in those early years.

What I like about math is that it is a way of describing the physical world. In fact, most major discoveries today are predicted mathematically before being proved empirically either in the lab or in nature. Good examples are Einstein's theory of relativity and the standard model of particle physics. The Standard Model, as it is called, mathematically predicts the existence of subatomic particles. From there, physicists go on to hunt for the particles by smashing protons together in large proton accelerators, such as CERN in Switzerland, thus revealing their subcomponents, which are amazingly consistent with what the mathematical model predicts.

Like the proton, the electron is part of this small, unseen world, and I had chosen an engineering major that had its basis in such particles. Math was the language that we learned to describe this unseen world and to manipulate it.

In line with my fascination with what was going on at the atomic level in the field of electrical engineering, I chose to write my senior paper on a phenomenon known as superconductivity. Superconductivity is electrons moving through certain materials that are maintained at very low temperatures, resulting in no resistance to their flow, a very handy phenomenon to work with in science and engineering. When I was in school in the late 1960s, there was no clear understanding of superconductivity or a consensus on what was going on at the atomic level. Some things scientists thought we understood and I wrote about in my senior paper have today been proven wrong or have been modified.

To this day, I continue to be keenly interested in particle physics for this reason. Particle physicists are still unlocking the mysteries of these fundamental building blocks of God's universe and apparently will be doing for some time to come.

College was supposed to be a time for obtaining a broad and mind-expanding liberal education beyond one's major, but most of my electives outside of engineering were used toward my goal of receiving a reserve commission in the United States Army and being an army officer as my father had been. I don't regret this, but I would have liked to have had more electives on the liberal arts side of things.

Chapter 5

1970—What a Year!

This was a salient year for Nancy and me.

Married in 1970: We were married on Labor Day weekend and had a brief honeymoon to Fripp Island. The father of the bride, Pete Cheetham, and my best man, my father, are shown in this picture. Another special picture during the wedding is that of our grandmothers (my grandchildren's great-great-grandmothers): Eva Friday Mann and Marguerite Catherine Hughes Cheetham. This is a cherished photograph.

Nancy's father, Pete Cheetham (left); Nancy; me;
my father, Peyton Hartley (right)

Grandmothers—Eva Mann (left) and Marguerite Cheetham (right)

A MEMORY THAT HAS stayed with Nancy and me over the years is our breakfast the first morning of our honeymoon: smoked salmon, bagels, cream cheese, onion, and capers. It has been our romantic special occasion breakfast ever since.

The honeymoon was short and rushed because I had just launched into my career as an electrical engineer with Duke Power Company in Charlotte, North Carolina. I had no way of taking much time off. We have made up for it since then with many wonderful getaways over the years.

Bachelor of science in electrical engineering: I received my undergraduate degree that same year, the culmination of four amazing years at Clemson.

Hired by Duke Power Company: My degree opened for me a wonderful career with Duke Power Company in power plant design engineering. Duke hired me right out of college knowing I had a two-year military obligation. I found this quite amazing. I spent about six months with Duke before being called on active duty, and I was assured my job with Duke would be waiting for me when I returned. This was a point of stability in the fast-moving, quick-changing next two years for Nancy and me.

Commission in the United States Army: Receiving a commission in the army, as my father had, was one of my earliest life goals. Although he talked about it very little, I knew of the great sacrifice my father made in World War II. I admired him and wanted to serve my country similarly; hence, I sought an army commission while at Clemson.

Chapter 6

The Army Days

In 1970, Nancy and I moved to Fort Gordon, Augusta, Georgia, for my training as a Signal Corps officer. This was a challenging six weeks for both of us but being in Augusta placed us close to Nancy's parents in Aiken, which made it a bit more enjoyable for us.

My original orders from there were to Fort Meade, Maryland, for further training before going to Vietnam. I was undaunted by the prospect of Vietnam. I simply considered it my duty and what I was supposed to do. In hindsight, I don't know why I wasn't more anxious about it.

It turned out, however, that my orders were changed. The top three people in our Signal Officers Basic Course at Fort Gordon were offered the opportunity to call Washington and get their orders changed. All thirty-five of us in the class were young lieutenants freshly out of college. No one was interested in doing more studying. I took advantage of that.

I FINISHED FOURTH IN my class, but an amazing thing happened. My classmate who finished third, having the assignment he wanted, went to our instructors and argued the case that I should have finished third. I didn't ask for this; he just did it, and I have no idea how he pulled it off. The rankings were changed. This was an amazing act of thoughtfulness for which I am grateful to this day.

Needless to say, it made a huge difference in the next two years for Nancy and me. I was given a number to call in Washington, and my orders were changed to a posting at Lexington Army Signal Depot in Kentucky. I worked on communications systems for the Strategic Communications Command in Germany for the rest of my active-duty time. It occasionally pricks my conscience, however, knowing that some other lieutenant probably went to Vietnam in my place.

Nancy and I enjoyed Kentucky. We had a duplex apartment on a quiet street that housed the junior officers assigned to the post. We were on a golf course with tennis courts right down the street, which was great since Nancy and I were big tennis players in those years. Perhaps the most enjoyable aspect was the officers club out our back door with fifteen-cent beers and inexpensive lunches.

We became good friends with many of the other young couples on post. They were from an array of places around the country, which made it interesting. Since I was traveling a great deal during that time to Germany for my work, I was gratified that Nancy was secure among some good new friends.

Nancy and I became particularly close friends with our next-door neighbors, Dennis and Sheila Wilson. Dennis was the provost marshal on post (responsible for security). He had crazy experiences flying Cobra gunships in Vietnam and had a crazy personality to match. We greatly enjoyed Dennis and Sheila.

Although my job in the army was interesting and challenging, it was also straightforward and stress free, different from my pending career with Duke and the rigors of starting a family, both of which we would soon be returning to.

Chapter 7

The Indian Land Years

We arrived back in Charlotte in 1973 just in time for Robin to be born. As a side note, we called him Robin throughout his younger years until, one day, he wanted to use the name "Rob." Nancy's father suggested that perhaps he was just tired of being named after a bird.

We bought a starter home in west Charlotte and in 1978 purchased four acres in Indian Land, Lancaster County, South Carolina, and built our home. Jimmy was born in 1979 just before we moved from Charlotte to Indian Land. The area was called Indian Land because, by a treaty with King George III in 1763, this area was originally designated for the Catawba Indians.

WHILE BUILDING THE HOUSE, I would work on it at night and on weekends, working during the day at Duke's uptown offices in Charlotte. It was a bit stressful, but the result was a wonderful home for our family. We lived in our beloved Indian Land home for the remainder of my thirty-one years with Duke, and it was where Rob and Jimmy grew into adulthood.

Robin (left), Jimmy (right)

OUR PROPERTY WAS WOODED, and a stream ran through the hollow at the back of the property. The whole area was largely woods and farmland back then, and the boys would range up and down that stream playing for hours at a time. Nancy's brother, Jim (James Larken Cheetham), wrote a poem for Robin one Christmas about how at the end of the day, the stream would "always bring him home."

Tennis was a big thing in the family, and that extended to Nancy's parents, Bobbie and Pete (Barbara Brown Cheetham and Joseph Eyre Larken Cheetham Jr.—note that you do not see "Pete" anywhere in that long name, but Pete was what he was called from his childhood). When the boys were in high school, I offered that, if either of them could beat me in a set of tennis, I would give them one hundred dollars. They didn't manage to do that then, but a few years ago, with me in my seventies, Jimmy wanted to know if the offer was still on.

IN OUR EARLY YEARS in Indian Land, my focus was on my career and providing for our family. It became a rather self-focused and myopic time for me. In 1980, the Lord challenged me on that. We were attending Saint Paul's Episcopal Church in Fort Mill, although we later would attend Christ Church in Lancaster. I was in the Saint Paul's churchyard on a Sunday morning. It was a beautiful fall morning with the large oak trees of the churchyard full of color. Nancy was off doing some ministry or another, and the boys were already in Sunday school. I was waiting to go into the adult class.

My conversation with God (don't worry—no audible voices) was about my convenient form of deism that kept God compartmentalized and uninvolved in most corners of my life. As a lifelong Christian, I knew that was not what my faith was supposed to look like. His place was at the center of my life, but that was where I was, and I figured it would get a bit crowded if God moved in. In my arrogance, I made a deal with the Lord about a trial period; I would see how things went. If one could make a deal with the devil, then I thought I ought to be able to make a deal with God. Looking back, I'm astounded at my condescension before God. Perhaps the towering oak trees protected me from a much-deserved lightning strike. From that point on, the Holy Spirit began to set my feet on a proper Christian path.

THIS WAS, HOWEVER, NOT happening in isolation. Nancy's brother, Jim, and our dear friends and fellow parishioners Tom and Gail shepherded us during this time. I would describe this as my born-again moment, as Jesus describes it to Nicodemus in John 3.[16]

This is the point in my life when Christianity began to make sense to me of this nonsensical world in which we live. Christianity had the answers to the first-order questions of life, like what is discussed in the prologue to this autobiography, such questions as

- "Who am I?"
- "Whose am I?"
- "From what or from whom do I derive my identity?"
- "For what purpose was I created?"
- "What is my ultimate *telos* and destiny?"

CHRISTIANITY, AS I WAS coming to understand it, was turning this upside-down world right side up for me.

This changed the trajectory of my life and Nancy's. My career was blessed by it; my marriage was blessed by it; my being a father to Rob and Jimmy was blessed by it. I was given a new life that brought joy, peace, and purpose. I began the proverbial journey from self-absorption to self-giving, a journey I'm still on to this day. Let me add that Nancy and I together made this journey into a more mature Christian faith, but my sense is that she was always out front and leading the way. I am hugely grateful to my dear wife for that.

The 1980s were, therefore, a time of growing in my knowledge, love, and service to God. Tithing became an honor as I began to learn how to give back to God. Cursillo (a three-day weekend retreat) taught me about being intentional and disciplined in my

---

16   John 3:1–16.

pursuit of God and the indispensable aspect of Christian community in doing that. My Cursillo small group, of which I was a part for twelve years at Christ Church, taught me about mutual support and accountability with fellow Christians, about growing in my relationship with God, and about being Christ to the world around me. This men's group became involved in Kairos Prison Ministry in the South Carolina state prison system, and I learned an enormous amount about working in the power of the Holy Spirit to make a difference in people's lives. I became lay rector (leader) of a weekend at Manning Correctional Institution with thirty inmates and fourteen volunteers—one of the toughest undertakings of my life. That weekend taught me immeasurably more about trusting God and simply stepping out and doing what He was calling me to do at the time.

In the early 1990s, a soon-to-be close friend, Doyle, was released from state prison and returned to Lancaster County. Doyle had a rocky upbringing, which led to his being incarcerated in the South Carolina Department of Juvenile Justice (DJJ) in Columbia and again later as an adult in the South Carolina Department of Corrections.

Doyle had attended Kairos in the Department of Corrections and, through one of our group members, was invited to be part of our men's group at Christ Church, Lancaster, when he returned home. Doyle wanted things to be different in his life, and God helped him with that. He became a solid Christian and eventually a part of the core leadership at Christ Church. He sought ways to give back to his community, to his new church family, and, most of all, to his fellow residents in both the adult prisons in the state and to the incarcerated youth in the DJJ from which he came.

Doyle, along with a few others in the state, had a vision of starting a ministry in the DJJ modeled on the Kairo adult ministry. It was called Epiphany. On the first Epiphany weekend in the DJJ, Doyle was the lay rector, and I was his coordinator (the person who took care of logistics and other details).

I was the lay rector of the next Epiphany weekend a few months later. What was extraordinarily special to me about that weekend was my sons, Rob and Jimmy, and a group of their friends from across our diocese, all college age or above at that time, joined with us to minister to these incarcerated and street-hardened boys of the DJJ. My sons and their friends went on to do a number of subsequent weekends. Their effectiveness was enhanced by the fact that they were only a few years older than these incarcerated teenagers. Among the greatest gifts they conveyed was hope—that is, the hope and the reality that life can be different and the hope that can be found in a relationship with their Creator. Nancy joined us in this ministry alongside her sons. I remember how hard she worked on those weekends and how she cared for those young people of the DJJ. It was a blessing for us all to be able to work with those incarcerated teenagers, to hear about their lives, and to tell them about ours.

Back on the home front, Nancy had been a good homemaker and the best of mothers to the boys. Rob had attended Indian Land School and Catawba Christian School in Rock Hill. He went on to Wofford College in Spartanburg, South Carolina. Jimmy graduated from Indian Land High School and attended the University of South Carolina in Columbia. While Nancy, rightfully so, was grieving over her empty nest, I was vicariously enjoying their college years with them. Our life in Indian Land was wonderful, Spirit filled, and full of blessings for Nancy, Rob, Jimmy, and me.

I thank God for those wonderfully rich years.

Robin and Jimmy

Chapter 8

My Career Designing Electrical Power Generating Stations

My office for many years was in the Duke Power building in uptown Charlotte (and later, out near the Charlotte airport). I was with Duke for a total of thirty-one years, from 1970 to 2001. Duke was an excellent company to work for, and the work was always interesting and challenging. I progressed in the company from my entry-level position as a junior engineer to middle management as an engineering manager over several power plant projects.

Fresh out of Clemson, I was assigned to work on Duke's nuclear power generating stations, all of which are still in service today— Oconee Unit 3, McGuire Units 1 and 2, and Catawba Unit 1. My expertise in those early days was main power system protection, metering, and control. I worked with engineers from many fine schools, mostly schools in the Southeast. I marveled at the proficiency the North Carolina State University engineers had at using a three-phase power system analysis tool known as "symmetrical components." I discovered later that the book we had used at Clemson was written by a professor all those engineers studied under at North Carolina State. They were just closer to the trough than I was.

McGuire Nuclear station[17]

IIT WAS MY PRIVILEGE to work alongside these fine engineers, many of whom became my closest friends in those years. As an engineering supervisor and later as an engineering manager, I hired many excellent engineers for Duke from the various schools they represented.

I also worked with design technicians/draftsmen who supported the engineers and turned engineering concepts into construction drawings. Most had technical college degrees, and Duke always hired the best. I marveled at how fast their jobs and the design process changed with the advent of the desktop computer. When I started at Duke, it would take about six designers to support one engineer. With the move from drafting table to computer-based drafting and integrated databases for material purchase and control, the efficiency of the technicians vastly increased. When I retired, the ratio was almost one to one, much to the credit of these technicians we engineers had the pleasure of working with.

---

17   Murr Rhame, "McGuire Nuclear Station from Lake Norman" (photo), Wikimedia Commons, April 14, 2013, https://commons.wikimedia.org/wiki/File:McGuire_Nuclear_Station_from_lake_Norman.jpg.

In addition to nuclear plants, I worked on coal-fired, natural gas, and hydroelectric power plants at various points in my career. I was also involved in the high-voltage substations connecting our power plants to the utility's power transmission grid.

The type of technology for generating electrical power that I favored was something called "combined-cycle power plants." Although they could also use oil, they typically used natural gas as a fuel to power very large gas turbines, not unlike oversized jet engines, to turn an electrical generator. The heat from the turbine exhaust would also be captured to make steam to further generate electricity, thus the term "combined-cycle." It was environmentally the cleanest and most efficient way to generate electricity from fossil fuels. It still is to this day.

Cope Plant[18]

I WAS THE LEAD electrical engineer on a number of projects during the 1980s and 1990s, but two of my favorites were Cope Generating Station, which we built for South Carolina Electric & Gas on the Edisto River in South Carolina, and the Batu Hijau project on the Indonesian island of West Nusa Tenggara.

---

18   Source: *The Times and Democrat.*

The final plant of my career was the Urquhart combined-cycle repowering project for South Carolina Electric & Gas Company. The Urquhart plant happens to be just downriver from our present home in North Augusta. When driving on the I-520 bypass around Augusta, I can see the stacks of the plant and am pleasantly reminded of my power plant design engineering days.

Urquhart Station[19]

NONE OF THESE PROJECTS, however, do I consider the pinnacle of my career. In 1998, I was approached by our vice president of operations about being the interim general manager of a power generation and transmission system we operated on the western end of the island of New Guinea. I had not worked on the engineering of that power system and was quick to inform operations that "I design 'em; I don't run 'em." That argument did not gain much traction among the higher-ups. The next thing Nancy and I knew, we were living in a little bungalow in the middle of the rain forests of New Guinea.

This assignment turned out to be both a great challenge and a great adventure. The power system I was to manage extended about seventy miles from the coast, where we

---

19   Source: https://www.gem.wiki/Urquhart_Station.

generated the bulk of our power, to the central mountains of New Guinea, near a four-teen-thousand-foot mountain from which our little Duke operating subsidiary derived its name, Puncakjaya Power. We called it "Pookie Power" for short.

The job had its challenges, both administratively and technically. One of the administrative challenges was I did not speak the language of at least 80 percent of the people working for the company. The largest technical challenge was the stability of the power system. In the United States, we are accustomed to being tied into all the power companies around us to help provide stability and reliable power flow. Pookie Power was all by itself in the middle of the New Guinean rain forest. The Indonesian engineers working for the company struggled to solve the problem. I was, however, the right guy to help with the stability difficulty. It took me all the way back to power system protection and control expertise of my junior engineer days.

New Guinea, Irian Jaya, and Pookie Power © 2022 TomTom

NANCY AND I FIT comfortably into the Duke team that managed this power system. It was a small contingent of about a dozen families, mostly from the Piedmont Carolinas, just like us. Nancy and I were committed to being unabashedly Christian in a predominately non-Christian place, and we found that it was also the case with most of the other expats we were working and living with. It was the Bible Belt coming out in all of us.

Nancy and I related well to everyone we encountered in Irian Jaya (the region by that name was a province of the country of Indonesia), but both of us describe it as a spiritually oppressive and dark place. As Nancy once remarked, "We're not in Kansas anymore, Toto." The dominant religion, at least politically and culturally, was Islam. The other large religious group was animism (nature worship) of the Melanesian people of that area. We found that our fellow Duke employees and their families were important in hedging us off spiritually from much of that.

I was amazed and proud at how well Nancy made the transition from raising our two boys in Indian Land, South Carolina, to living in the middle of a rain forest and relating to all the very different people around her. My favorite story is of her and the yard boy she hired from among the local indigenous tribe. His name was Yaki. Yaki was not very dependable and had no trace of what one would call a Western work ethic. Nancy ended up firing Yaki. We all held our breath to see how Yaki and his tribe would take that. We knew them to be a fractious and volatile people.

I witnessed their volatility on my very first week in Irian Jaya. We lived just about in the center of the seventy-mile-long power system. On my first drive to the coast to visit the large power-generating plant we had there, I parked beside the river where I was going to catch a boat to the plant. (Water was the only way one could get to it.) A large crowd of local men who lived on stilt houses in the river had gathered at the boat landing. They were jumping up and down and chanting something. My first thought was that it was a pep rally for a soccer match or some other sporting event. I found my way through the crowd and to the awaiting boat on the river. The boat operator informed me that the local men were getting revved up to go to war with another village inland over the honor of a young girl from their village. I immediately thought of what Nancy said: "We're not in Kansas anymore, Toto."

My trips inland to the other end of the power system were equally adventurous. I had a Toyota four-wheel drive, supercharged diesel truck to use. On my first trip into the mountains, I quickly found out why I needed such a powerful truck. Driving about twenty miles from our bungalow on dirt roads through the rain forest, I came to the mountains that rose abruptly out of the rain forest. The procedure, as explained to me, was to stop, put the truck in four-wheel drive, and head up the mountain, keeping the RPMs up and hoping to get to the top before the supercharger overheated. It was the steepest road I had ever driven on and unquestionably the most dangerous.

My office at that end of the system was in a mining camp at about twelve-thousand-foot elevation. The place was often shrouded in clouds and always wet and chilly. It made things surreal. The fact that I traveled up the mountain and back several times a week led to lethargy from altitude sickness, which added to the whole surreal experience.

At the time we left Irian Jaya, there was unrest and rioting occurring in Jakarta, the Indonesian capital. That would have been our normal route home, but prudence dictated that we go home another way. My secretary at the mining camp managed to get us on a mining company transport plane to Guam. The flight was unfortunately delayed until after midnight when our visas expired. There we were, stuck at a vintage World War II airstrip in the middle of the night, in the middle of a jungle, speaking the wrong language. Yet another surreal Irian Jaya experience! Fortunately, I knew the customs official on duty from bringing workers to the island, and by passing an ample amount of Duke's cash across the table, we were able to board the plane to Guam.

Duke management, in appreciation of us having taken this rather odd assignment, told Nancy and me to be in no hurry getting back in Charlotte. We spent time on Guam and the Hawaiian Islands. Eventually flying to San Francisco, we rented a car and drove up the Pacific coast. In Seattle, we finally boarded a flight to Charlotte.

We missed our family while in Irian Jaya, and it's good to know that they perhaps missed us too. Our younger son, Jimmy, was at the University of South Carolina at the time, and he would send forlorn emails about how he had been orphaned. He left home for school, and his parents moved away. He had heard about such things—but moving eleven time zones away was a little excessive. My brother said he wanted to visit and wanted to know how to get there. I told him it was easy: "Just go to Singapore and take a left."

I look back on Irian Jaya, albeit a short assignment, as the zenith of my career both technically and managerially. It was also a fantastic adventure, although I'm sure that's not the way Nancy would describe it.

Part III

The Mature Years

Chapter 9

God's Plan

My thirty-one-year career with Duke from junior engineer to middle management was challenging and fulfilling, and I'm blessed by those years. I made good friends at Duke and was saddened in year 2000 to be considering leaving that wonderful career behind.

Through the mid-1990s, I had been taking courses at Trinity Seminary (Trinity Episcopal School for Ministry) in Ambridge, Pennsylvania. These were interterm intensive courses in which I did assigned reading in advance of going to the Trinity campus, followed by one week of intensive classes for the required contact hours with the professor, and then completing the course with paper writing over the next six weeks. I typically did this twice a year in January and June. Being on the Trinity campus was always a welcomed time of retreat and spiritual refreshment. I would leave behind my job in Charlotte and spend a week in a very different environment focused on very different topics.

On our return trip from Irian Jaya, while flying from Guam to Hawaii, Nancy and I talked about my entering the discernment process for Holy Orders (the priesthood) and moving to seminary full time. It was a year later and after much prayer that Nancy and I decided we would do it. I therefore retired from Duke in 2001.

Our two boys were now grown men and, at this point, would be unaffected by the pending change in their parents' life. A great blessing was Duke had paid me well over the years, and if we made no more money for the rest of our lives, we would have all we needed. To be able to do this at age fifty-three was a God thing. The Lord had generously given to us, and now we had the opportunity to give back in a unique way.

My bishop, however, did not allow me to continue my studies at Trinity Seminary, and he wanted me to consider other schools. He deemed Trinity Seminary too traditional and theologically conservative for the modern-day Episcopal priesthood. My church history and systematic theology courses I had taken at Trinity spent a great deal of time on this shift taking place in many quarters of the contemporary church. This shift is to modernist Christianity and away from historic apostolic faith. The Episcopal Church was thus rapidly becoming a different church from the one in which I had come to know the Lord. I knew well what my bishop was talking about and could not disagree that I might be too theologically conservative and traditional for the Episcopal priesthood. This brought on another decision point for Nancy and me.

Our decision was to press on toward my calling. I had completed enough hours at Trinity to receive a diploma in Anglican studies. I then enrolled, with my bishop's permission, at the Lutheran Seminary in Columbia, South Carolina, to complete my work toward a Master of Divinity degree. The Lutheran Seminary provided the added advantage of keeping me physically located in the diocese and connected with my current lay ministries. It also kept Nancy and me close to our younger son's family and our extended family.

While in seminary and later as an ordained deacon after seminary, I was assigned to the Church of the Good Shepherd in Columbia. The bishop felt it would be good for me to have some exposure to the Anglo-Catholic side of Anglicanism to balance my Evangelical past. I was very glad to do that. I must state, however, that even having attended an

Evangelical seminary, I didn't feel I had been formed in one direction or the other of the two traditional forms of Anglican worship, and I still don't to this day.

The rector at Good Shepherd was an old friend, and I was delighted to have him as my mentor for a season. Additionally, and apparently unknown to my bishop, Good Shepherd was my mother's church during World War II and while she was studying at the University of South Carolina. It was also the church in which both my brother Dan and I were baptized. How's *that* for coming full circle?

Chapter 10

Vicar of Saint John's

During my time as an ordained deacon at the Church of the Good Shepherd, the bishop asked me to pastor the small struggling congregation of Saint John's, Clearwater, near North Augusta, South Carolina. The bishop was considering closing Saint John's and wanted my opinion.

THE DOORS OF THE church were being kept open by a small clutch of elderly ladies. A delightful retired priest living in the area was celebrating Holy Eucharist for them on Sundays, and that did not change with my arrival. The bishop did not approve of "Deacon's Masses" in which bread and wine were consecrated by a priest elsewhere and distributed at Sunday service by a deacon. I was fine with this and focused on preaching, teaching, and pastoral visiting; besides, I enjoyed working alongside my older retired friend.

After several months, I gave the bishop an answer to his question. I said the congregation had great potential and the church should not be closed. He responded by assigning me as their new vicar. Is it not just like that in every organization when you volunteer an opinion? I was soon ordained to the priesthood and spent the next six years in that delightful little church.

Saint John's had suffered over the years from the lack of a full-time pastoral presence, and their numbers had dwindled. Having found the old parish roles, I systematically got to know various lapsed members as well as meet others in the Clearwater area. The church began to grow. You can see how hard I worked at that from the picture below.

Hardworking Vicar of Saint John's

THE PEOPLE OF THE surrounding community were wonderful but generally faced significant challenges. Saint John's was in Horse Creek valley, also known as Midland Valley, in Aiken County, South Carolina. The valley was at one time lined with textile mills and small textile towns. Clearwater was one of those mill towns. As happened throughout the South, textile mills slowly disappeared, leaving small communities without their mills and few other means of livelihood. Clearwater had more than its share of elderly people financially locked in place and young people struggling to find work. This led to an elevated drug scene and a rise in petty crime across Midland Valley.

Clearwater's situation, however, made it a place with plenty of pastoral ministry opportunities. A case in point: I became friends with a man who grew up in the valley and had suffered from all its social and economic woes. He and his two adult daughters were addicted to prescription drugs, and he obviously had a successful way for obtaining those drugs. He and I had many conversations about this.

One morning, he called me and asked if I would come by. He met me in his driveway with a sack full of pills, handed them to me, and submitted to my taking him to get some help. He was admitted to a rehab program that proved ultimately a success for him. A few days later, I recalled the sack of pills still in my glove compartment. I was horrified that I had been driving around town with those pills in my possession. I quickly destroyed them.

At one level, the drugs, alcohol, and damaged lives in Midland Valley seemed overwhelming. Being pastorally involved in people's lives allowed me to see this firsthand. I did manage to make a difference in some lives, and I thank God for that. The sad part is that it was only a drop in the bucket. I am, however, comforted by what is called the "starfish story:"

There were hundreds of starfish washed up on the beach following a storm, and a man was walking along, stooping down, picking up starfish one by one, and hurling them out over the breakers back into the sea. Another man, watching, approached him and questioned, "There are hundreds, maybe even thousands of starfish stranded on this beach. How can you possibly make a difference?"

The man stooped down, picked up yet another starfish, hurled it into the sea and said, "It made a difference to that one."

IT WAS DURING MY seminary years and my time at Saint John's that two wonderful events took place in our life. Our two sons were married: Rob and Sabrina in 2002 and Jimmy and Caroline a few years later. It's hard to express how blessed we were to have these two new daughters-in-law come into our lives.

Rob and Sabrina met at Christ Church, Lancaster, when Sabrina came to the area as a music teacher in the local school system. She joined the choir of which Rob was a member, and they were soon making beautiful music together (pardon the old, worn-out cliché). Rob and Sabrina were married at Christ Church by the Reverend Bill Walters, who was Rob's priest through much of his growing-up years. Rob honored me by asking me to be his best man. Rob and Sabrina soon moved to Northern Virginia where they have lived, worked, and raised our beloved granddaughter, Katherine. Building on his Wofford education, Rob obtained an MBA degree from George Mason University and has developed a successful career in commercial real estate in the Washington–Baltimore area.

Jimmy (left), Nancy's Mother Bobbie, Sabrina, Rob, Nancy, Me (right)

JIMMY AND CAROLINE MET at Camp Gravatt,[20] a place cherished by both to this day. Jimmy had finished at the University of South Carolina with a degree in religion. (My standard and somewhat inappropriate comment to him back then was, "I didn't know they had religion at USC"). He became the youth minister at Saint Bartholomew's Episcopal Church in North Augusta. Caroline moved to Charleston to attend the College of Charleston and later the Medical University of South Carolina. When Caroline departed for Charleston, Jimmy, without hesitation, resigned from his youth minister position at Saint Bart's to move to Charleston and continue the courtship (we all knew where this was headed). Jimmy is one of those young men who always seems to land on his feet, and it turned out that Sonny Goldston, Caroline's father, gave him a contact for a job writing reports for a soils testing laboratory in the Charleston area. He got the job and was appar-

---

20   Gravatt Camp and Conference Center is an Episcopal center in Aiken County, South Carolina.

ently pretty good at it—until Grace Episcopal Church, a large downtown church on the Charleston peninsula, offered him a position as their youth minister.

Jimmy and Caroline were married at Grace Church, and I had the great joy and honor of being a co-officiant at their wedding. Their gift to me was a white priest stole, which I wore at their wedding and treasure to this day.

Sabrina (left), Rob, Bobbie, Caroline, Jimmy, Nancy, Me (right)

CAROLINE WENT ON TO do a yearlong dental residency at the University of Alabama at Birmingham. Upon moving to Birmingham, the soils testing laboratory in Charleston offered Jimmy his old job back and offered to send him a computer and software to do his old job from Birmingham. Did I mention that Jimmy seemed to always land on his feet? Delightfully, and in addition, Jimmy's best and closest friend from their growing-up years, Tommy Goodwin, happened to live in Birmingham.

Tommy and Jimmy on the Catawba River in their slightly younger years

FROM THERE JIMMY AND Caroline moved to Columbia, South Carolina, where Caroline entered a dental practice and Jimmy continued to do soils testing report-writing from home.

It was during this time in Columbia that grandsons William and Robert would be arriving on the scene. William was born on July 17, 2010 and Robert on November 13, 2012.

It was also during this time that Jimmy began the discernment process for Holy Orders in the Episcopal Church, a natural trajectory from his youth ministry experience. They were soon off to Virginia Theological Seminary (VTS) in Alexandria, Virginia. It pleased Nancy and me that Rob and Jimmy were now geographically back close together, at least for the three years of Jimmy's seminary training. We enjoyed driving up for visits and getting to see both boys and their families.

Another thing that pleased me greatly was Jimmy asking me to review the papers he wrote for his various classes at VTS. I vicariously lived through seminary once again and learned much from Jimmy and his seminary writings.

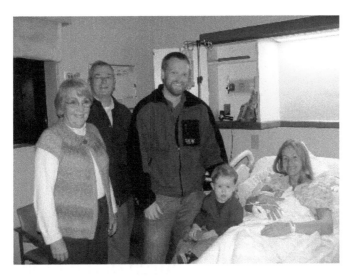

Robert's birth

JIMMY COMPLETED HIS MASTER of Divinity degree, and then his family went back to Columbia. Caroline reestablished herself in a dental practice, and Jimmy became the deacon at Church of the Good Shepherd in Columbia. You may recall from chapter 9 that I was also assigned to that very same church—different Hartley, same church. Considering that his grandmother attended there, his father (me) was baptized there, and his father (me) had previously served as ordained deacon there, I loved the connection.

Jimmy went on to be on the staff of Saint David's in Columbia, where he was ordained to the priesthood. During this time, Caroline and Jimmy gave birth to our precious granddaughter Sinclair on October 21, 2016. Jimmy went on to serve on the bishop's staff for several years before moving into his current position as a canon at Trinity Cathedral, Columbia.

Chapter 11

Planting the Anglican Church of the Holy Trinity

I enjoyed my time at Saint John's, Clearwater, but I realized more and more that it was necessary that it come to an end. I had seen many changes growing up in the Episcopal Church, but my beloved church was in the middle of the theological shift of which I, at last, concluded I could neither follow nor ignore. This had been an issue when I was pursuing Holy Orders, and now, five years into my ordained ministry, I felt it was time to again talk to the bishop about it.

I made an appointment, drove to Columbia, and voiced my concerns under two overarching topics. The first was the primacy of the "apostolic deposit" (the witness of the apostles codified in sacred Scripture). The trend in the wider church was the normalizing of the belief that Scripture should be trumped by modern reason and cultural norms, something with which I was struggling.

My second overarching concern was our going soft on and moving away from the uniqueness of the incarnate Christ (Christ alone) to save us from ourselves by the propitiation for our sins and the undoing of our estrangement from God. This is at the heart of our Trinitarian understanding of God and of Jesus as the second person of the Trinity, God Incarnate. We had a presiding bishop at the time who was open in challenging John

14:6, which is Jesus declaring that He is "the Way, the Truth, and the Life." I understood her feelings that such a theology was limiting to God, but, in my eyes, it expresses man's limitation, not God's; besides, Jesus says it and I know it to be true. We ourselves do not have the ability to make things right with God. We need God to do for us what we cannot do for ourselves. I respect people committed to other faith systems, but Christianity is the only thing that makes sense of this world and the persistent evil in it. These were indelible beliefs for both the primitive church and the Reformation church with which we are in continuity, and they are indelible beliefs to me. I concluded that, indeed, I would not make a very good priest in the contemporary Episcopal Church.

The bishop was cordial and understanding and said he would accept my resignation when I was ready. This visit with him was in early 2008. In January 2009, I sent my letter of resignation with a month's notice, although I knew he would not accept the month's notice as it was not the current practice of the Episcopal Church to do so.

Since I clearly wanted to continue in Holy Orders in the Anglican Church, albeit now outside the Episcopal Church, I contacted the Anglican Province of Nigeria, asking to come under that bishop's authority. Anglican polity, as it is in most churches, is that a presbyter (priest) is always under the authority of a bishop. After submitting the appropriate paperwork, I was informed that, concurrent with offering my resignation to my current bishop, I would be canonically resident in the Anglican Province of Nigeria.

A group of laypeople, along with one other clergyman and myself, planned the establishment of an Anglican Church in North Augusta. The Anglican Church of the Holy Trinity was born on the First Sunday after the Feast of the Epiphany in January 2009. It was a great celebration, and our temporary facility was wall-to-wall with people. Many were new parishioners but also well-wishers from around the Central Savannah River Area.

The core lay leadership of Holy Trinity and I knew I-20 exit 5 (known as the Sweetwater Community) was the right place to plant a church. Aiken County's growth corridor was projected to be from exit 1 (the first exit out of Georgia) to exit 16. Exit 5 is right in the middle. We thus established a one-year lease in a temporary facility in the Sweetwater area of North Augusta.

At the end of that first year, the vestry went on retreat at a parishioner's beach house at Hilton Head. The big topic of discussion was our space problem. We had, in fact, outgrown our facilities immediately after the onset of our church plant. The vestry was aware of a building available very near us. We hashed through the financial and logistical details of moving there, prayed about it, hopped in our cars, and headed back to North Augusta to make it happen.

AS IT TURNED OUT, this was taking place in the middle of an economic recession. Economic growth in the area had stalled, and commercial property owners around us were hungry for cash. This made it possible to get a good deal on the building as well as purchase four additional acres. God provided for us in those early years in many ways, and this was one of them.

ALTHOUGH HOUSING AND NEW families had also stalled during this time, we continued to expand our numbers and fund our internal and outreach ministries. We were never too poor not to put money and resources back into the community and into foreign missions.

Spiritual formation was a priority at Holy Trinity. My sense was that our mainline churches of all stripes had focused too little on adult spiritual formation in that if one does not know the truth of the Gospel and teachings of the one, holy, catholic,[21] and apostolic church, one is open to believing anything. This was a time when many even considered the core doctrines of the faith inappropriate, divisive, and counter to inclusiveness.

---

21   catholic means "universal," and the small c differentiates the word from a denomination's name, the Roman Catholic Church.

TEACHING THE HISTORIC FAITH and Trinitarian Christianity was a priority in my rectorship both at Saint John's and Holy Trinity. Even the name Holy Trinity was selected with this in mind. It was not proposed by me but one of our laypeople who understood the significance of God having revealed Himself as Trinity of Persons. Often in history, heresies have happened by the church simply straying from a clear understanding of the Trinity—more precisely, by either discounting or denying Jesus's divinity, or discounting or denying His humanity. A useful exposition on this can be found in The Right Reverend C. FitzSimons Allison's book *The Cruelty of Heresy*.[22]

Time under our Nigerian bishop turned out to be short. In 2009, the same year we planted Holy Trinity, churches such as ours across the US and Canada came together with the encouragement of a number of Anglican provinces worldwide to form a province of churches known as the Anglican Church in North America (ACNA). The ACNA, of course, formed itself into dioceses, and Holy Trinity initially found itself part of a diocese centered around Atlanta. Dioceses continued to form, however, and several years later, we became part of the newly formed Diocese of the Carolinas.

---

22   Allison, *The Cruelty of Heresy* (Morehouse Publishing, 1994).

The Lord greatly blessed me and the people of Holy Trinity during these years. It was in 2019, ten years into my rectorship, that I informed my bishop that the parish needed a younger, more high-energy priest. The vestry called just such a person, and I retired in 2019 at age seventy-two.

Anglican Church of the Holy Trinity

ONE OF THE MOST cherished memories in my priesthood is my retirement supper and celebration at the church. The people I had come to dearly love told of their love and appreciation of me. I was humbled and gratified, but most of all, I was blessed to see a parish hall packed full of people representing a healthy congregation ready to continue doing the work the Lord had commissioned His Church to do.

Chapter 12

Retiring at Our Beloved Oakhurst Drive Home

Retiring as rector of Holy Trinity didn't mean I was retiring from the priesthood. The priesthood is simply not something from which one retires. At ordination, the ordinand is doing something—namely, taking vows and accepting a specific role to be played in God's church. But God is also doing something; He is calling that person, setting that person apart, and equipping the ordinand for ministry. God is making the ordinand a priest in His church by empowering, equipping, and changing the ordinand to live into the call by the indwelling power of His Holy Spirit. In God's great economy of things, ordination is thus an ontological event in which one's very nature is changed. I am, therefore, indelibly a priest and will continue to function as a priest to the extent I'm able and when called upon. This is not unlike baptism, in which God calls us out of the world to be a new creation and become citizens of the Kingdom of Heaven. We are given a new identity and new destiny.

Upon retiring, my priority was to stay out of the way of the new rector. Nancy and I had the perfect solution: an around-the-world cruise. It turned out to be a halfway-around-the-world cruise because the COVID-19. The pandemic struck, ending our vacation. It was, nonetheless, a wonderful time, and we got to see many places we would never have gotten to see otherwise. We traveled with our daughter-in-law's parents, Polly and Sonny Goldston, which made it doubly enjoyable. We met the Goldstons during Caroline and Jimmy's courtship and have been close friends ever since.

Our Almost Around-the-world Cruise with Polly and Sonny

WHETHER WE WOULD AT some point return to Holy Trinity and reengage with that church family remained to be seen at this point. It, of course, depended on the wishes of the new rector. It also depended my ability to stay out of new rector's running of the church. Since Holy Trinity is the only ACNA church around this area, returning to Holy Trinity was something we wanted to explore.

Upon returning to North Augusta from our travels and after conversations with the new rector, I reengaged with the parish and made myself pastorally available as a resident priest and the retired founding rector. As I've been able, I have taken on pastoral ministry to some of our homebound and those in the hospital and tended to various other pastoral needs within the parish. That was perfect in that it played into my first love during my active priesthood, which was pastoral care and counseling.

We knew our Oakhurst Drive home would be a comfortable place for our retirement years, but the house is too large for just Nancy and me. It turns out, however, to be the perfect place to have our grandchildren stay, especially in the summer with the pool in the backyard. The boys have their room upstairs, and the girls have theirs.

All too soon, however, they'll all be in their busy teens with interests other than coming to grandmommy and granddaddy's house, but the four of them will always be welcome here.

THE YARD IS SEVERAL acres, and I enjoy being outside taking care of the grass and gardens. I have been cutting grass and trimming hedges since I was our grandsons' age.

Here in 2022, my pilgrimage is far from over. Enjoying our home, enjoying our children and grandchildren, and enjoying our friends fills our time. My bicycle riding continues to bring enjoyment. The North Augusta Greeneway (spelled with the extra *e* because it's named after a former city mayor by that name) is a beautiful place to exercise. It's a railroad bed converted to a walking and biking trail that runs down off the Piedmont of upper South Carolina, through the city of North Augusta, and down into the Savannah River valley. My 10.5-mile routine a couple times a week never gets old. I enjoy the Greeneway particularly in the summer at first light. It gives me time with the Lord as I ride and enjoy His beautiful creation.

A thing I'm intentional about on the Greeneway is greeting the people I pass. At my age, I'm not riding so fast that I don't have time to speak, and it's a good Southern tradition with which I grew up. Besides, one never knows if you are passing a person who could use a friendly greeting.

Admittedly, only a retired person with plenty of time to think about such things would do this, but I calculated how many people I've greeted over my nineteen years of bicycling on the North Augusta Greeneway. I did the math[23] and figure I have greeted fifty-five thousand people, plus or minus four percent. This is almost twice the current population of North Augusta. This is also one way some folk around town got to know me as the pastor at the "Angel-ican church," which is the way it often gets pronounced.

Let me close this chapter with a word about my extended family, all of whom have been of great importance in my life. We now have two generations who have come after mine, and that translates into a lot of first, second, and third cousins. Thanksgiving celebrations and oyster roasts at my brother Dan's and sister-in-law Pat's home in Mount

---

23   Nineteen years × two rides per week (average) × fifty-two weeks × twenty-eight people per ride (average, not counting babies in strollers) = 55,328 people.

Pleasant have been the major gathering for the Hartley clan through the years. We also have opportunities to gather with the Cheetham clan, such as spending a week with all the Cheetham children and their children at Kanuga a few years back.

Chapter 13

The Joy of Grandparenthood

And what a delightful time of life this is! Nancy and I are part of our grandchildren's lives as much as we possibly can be. As mentioned in the previous chapter, we love having them stay with us in the summers, and we go to their events when we can. In it all, it has been a joy watching them grow and flourish.

Our sons and their wives are extraordinarily good parents, which has been a blessing to watch, and each child is thriving in their own way and with their own set of attributes. Katherine, the oldest grandchild, is beautiful, smart, interested in all kinds of things, full of questions, and always seeking answers. William is happy, good-natured, driven yet kind. Robert is intense, full of imagination, and a quite a joy to be with, and it's an honor to have him as my namesake. Sinclair, at five years old at of the writing of this history, is a loving, smart, perceptive, discerning little girl. She is also very much her own person. That's a way of saying she's headstrong and determined, which are traits that can take her far in life. It's going to be fun watching Sinclair grow up.

In recent years, Nancy and I have been taking the grandchildren individually on special trips to special places. There are too many to chronicle in any depth in this autobiography, but we have great memories of being with Katherine in New York City and Williamsburg, and are hoping to do something special with her as she finishes high school and moves toward college.

WE'VE BEEN TO MOUNT Rushmore and Yosemite with William. We made these trips with my brother Dan, his wife Pat, and their granddaughter Carsten Galetolie. These two cousins, William and Carsten, are close in age and the best of friends. Their friendship reminds me of the close cousin-to-cousin relationship of William's dad, Jimmy, and Carsten's mother, Peyton, when they were their children's age.

WE ATTEMPTED TO TAKE William and Carsten to Yellowstone, but the national park flooded from heavy rains and had to close about the time we were set to go. We instead did "Camp Hartley" at Dan and Pat's home in Mount Pleasant. Dan did a great job planning a week's worth of adventures for the two cousins, such as an excursion up the Intracoastal Waterway, crabbing, exploring Morris Island, and more.

Our first trip with Robert was to Dollywood and the Cherokee Indian Reservation in the Smoky Mountains. We have since taken him to Saint Augustine, Cape Canaveral, Sedona Red Rock Country, and the Grand Canyon. We did an amazing twenty-eight-mile whitewater boat adventure with Robert through the Grand Canyon on the Colorado River, and I survived to write about it.

MY HOPE IS TO build many more such memories with these grandchildren. Sinclair is just approaching the age where she can go on her own set of adventures. Being with Sinclair is an adventure in itself.

Epilogue

Perhaps it is presumptuous to think someone might care to hear about my pilgrimage through life. It does seem, however, that a grandfather who has lived the biblical threescore and ten years ("and if by reason of strength they be fourscore years," as the psalmist adds[24]) should tell his story to his grandchildren who are just starting on their pilgrimage through life. I think it is a gift worth giving to them.

I titled my life history *Under God's Umbrella* because of the strong sense I have that my whole life has been sheltered under the umbrella of God's bountiful grace and providence. I have stepped out from under that umbrella time and again only to have the Lord invite me back under to give me yet another dose of His love and mercy.

I have been blessed by God and pray the same for my grandchildren. May they have every bit of joy in life that Nancy and I have received, and more.

---

24   Psalm 90:10.

About the Author:

ROBERT MANN HARTLEY is a graduate of Clemson University with a BS in electrical engineering. After 31 years in power plant design engineering, he retired to attend Trinity School for Ministry (Anglican) and Lutheran Theological Southern Seminary. Following ordination, Robert assisted at Church of the Good Shepherd in Columbia, SC, and was vicar of St. John's Episcopal Church in Clearwater, SC, prior to becoming the founding rector of the Anglican Church of the Holy Trinity, North Augusta, SC. Robert is now retired and resides in North Augusta with his wife, Nancy. They have two sons, Rob and Jimmy and four grandchildren, Katherine, William, Robert, and Sinclair.